The Architecture of Chance

Christodoulos Makris

Wurm Press, 77 Kilnacourt, Portarlington
Co Laois, Ireland

ISBN: 978-0-9563732-9-8

Cover design: Adrian Reid
orange-ade@hotmail.com

Acknowledgements

3:AM Magazine, The Ash Wednesday series, *A Telmetale Bloomnibus* (Irish Writers' Centre), *BRAND, Burning Bush II, cancan, Colony, Genius or Not, gorse, The Guardian, Herbarium, Neither Use nor Ornament, Neon Highway, New Planet Cabaret* (New Island/RTÉ), *nth position, Occupy Writers, Penduline, Poetry Salzburg Review, Rain of Poems* (Casagrande), *ROPES* (NUI Galway), *Round the Clock* (Wurm Press), *Succour, UpStart, VLAK, The World Record* (Bloodaxe).

'Why I live in Egypt' was commissioned by Nick Pearson as a response to/commentary on his art practice for a monograph on his work.

'Metro Herald's Advertorial Wind Bags Let Loose, 28-31 May & 4-7 June 2013' was commissioned by The Irish Writers' Centre's Clodagh Moynan as a contemporary response to the 'Aeolus' episode in James Joyce's *Ulysses*.

public-private from 'Public Announcement' was commissioned by SJ Fowler for the fourth in his 'Camarade' series of events (Rich Mix arts centre, London, 9 February 2013).

'Safe as Houses' was made into a short film with support from Speaking Volumes Live Literature Productions.

*

Website: http://yesbutisitpoetry.blogspot.com

Twitter: @c_makris

Contents

We can distinguish two types of cityscape: those which are formed deliberately, and others which develop unintentionally. The former derive from the artistic will that is realised in squares, vistas, arrangements of buildings, and effects of perspective which Baedeker generally illuminates with a star. The latter on the other hand come into being without having been planned in advance. They are not compositions like Pariser Platz or La Concorde which owe their existence to a single architectural conception, rather they are creations of chance, which cannot be accounted for. Wherever a mass of stone and lines of streets, whose components result from completely different interests, come together, there you will find this kind of cityscape, which has never been the focus of any interest as such. It is no more designed than nature itself, and resembles a landscape in that it asserts itself unconsciously. Without a thought for how it appears, it slumbers through time.

Siegfried Kracauer
Seen from the Window (*Aus den Fenster Gesehen*)
trans. Lyn Marven

Scales

Another black coffee delivers exhilaration, fingers go haywire instantly. Jazzed kangaroo lawyers mesmerise novices, openly parroting queens. Randy sailors turn uninitiated vicars, whip xenophobes, yodel zanily.

Zoning yellowed x-rays with violet undertones throughout seems risky. Queuing patiently over night might leave knackered joints. Important: hold gamely. Fleeing early doors can't be advised.

Altar boys come delayed. Elderly foreigners gazump high infidels just kissing. Later, moustachioed nationalists officially publish quibbles, reciprocate. Sensing trouble, unstable volunteers write x yelling zugzwang.

Zoology yields xerographic work. Voicing unease, tired sophomores retract questions. Parents odiously networking more leverage, kowtow. Janitors investigate honorary guests. Females elope, defying common betrothal agendas.

Assist burly constables during erotic fanfares. Go hunting illegally. Jeer kettled lovebirds. Meet new orators praising quangos. Read speeches totally undermining visiting workers, x-rated yogis, zithers.

Zero year xmas went viral: unnameable tribes seeking ratification qualified poetry's objectives. Nobody mentioned liberty. Knowing journalists inadvisably halted gleeful fictions. Erstwhile desperate capitalists banked again.

Metro Herald's Advertorial Wind Bags Let Loose, 28-31 May & 4-7 June 2013

Silicon republic has named Dublin an innovation. Screw money, you can eat data. Free buses, food banks, meal services every other day. I received funny looks in a pub in Spain when I asked for an Irish breakfast. If they want to call it an English breakfast why sign it an Ulster one? The great looking dark Irishman should be adopted now, free installation and no deposit. This has happened recently to six of my friends. Two youths bought me a Cosmo and gave me a cigarette to get over the shock.

I couldn't agree more with James from Swords. Do people really need to be sexually stimulated every time they walk – you were wearing tight shorts and a lovely pair – what are the repercussions of this constant and obvious stimulation on our society, particularly when it goes unnourished? Treatment in our state of the art facilities in Budapest with free accommodation, discount on all private services. Customers resident in the island of Ireland are advised to submit their applications to book an appointment to roll out the appointments system in the coming months. We reserve the right to limit your service, some exclusions may apply. Send us your Instagram and Hipstamatic. Check out this strapping fellow. An Irish one would have a third sausage.

If you are involved in a community or voluntary group raising community spirit in your area we could help your dance moves to Is This The Way To Amarillo. Flashes of lemon, lime and orange will carry you through. Tell us in no more than 100 words why you deserve to be customers. By texting you're consenting to work easy, play hard and connect. Provider is Bank of Ireland. It was announced on Twitter big girls get a raw deal. Model is shown for illustrative purposes only. I told staff at Balbriggan, who said it couldn't be changed.

To celebrate 50 years in Ireland there was a signal failure at Merrion. On Tuesday evening the DART was stuck in Bray, I caught you looking back at me when you got off and you told me to commit suicide. Another story in the news that the Irish drink too much. Please, we teach French courses, help build homes with local families, drink sensibly, watch Argentina. Our most powerful citizens were regarded as being able to walk on water. Jesus Christ always lets you know how much gas you've used.

Please recycle this Metro Herald. I've tried online, and experienced some degree of success writing a novel. Have you considered drink-driving, violence, teenage pregnancy, antisocial behaviour? It's a time bomb for the online community who love telling us all about themselves and their lifestyles, those teenagers who ran riot at Portmarnock beach. Those who are tourists – the announcement will be lost on them anyway – rush out and buy that Joyce coin. Someone obviously thought it didn't look Oirish enough and stuck on a fada. Do you know both Michael Collins and Linda Martin are trending at the moment in Danish and European hospitals?

A young boy learns that he has extraordinary powers and is not of this earth because their great great great great uncle twice removed through marriage was related to some O'Cruises in Leitrim or some other godforsaken hole. Sound like fun? Excellent performance crackles a tremendous tour de force production. Feelings of stress, worry, anxiety of Tesco staff and customers nationwide preparing our graduates for the real world where Tubridy or that Herman Munster look-a-like joke I had a sick baby. We are giving Metro Herald readers the opportunity to learn Spanish, purchase a luxurious long Swedish body #isthatathing?

Summer has literally sprung upon us. Irish owned and operated, it now ranks as the most convoluted system in the EU. Stone cold stylish compelling gritty, made in sweatshop. In France they have barred bankers, developers and politicians. New airbrush USA summer available now handles pregnancy pouch and back, stubborn fat from tummy, massive legs. A woman flung the MetroH off a randomers face on the DART. You may, as a newspaper, write about current popular culture, but you really did not need to use such a sizeable image, a pointless page filler.

You know how much gas you've used? Sometimes the window nearly shatters, one day it will go through. Gas, all the big child adults moaning. Lol, lol, lol. Utterly hilarious gloriously entertaining the outrageous true history's greatest scumbags long been allowed to rule the roost in Dublin. I'd much rather my taxes be spent on thugs. I'd rather staple my nipples to an electricity pole and hang upside down all day than avoid reading all the tweets and Facebook posts. Can everyone who is unemployed or retired stay out of city centres?

The Impressionists

Round them up, the Impressionists,
even those straddling the margins
of their place and time – idealists
prone to self-harm, hermits opting
to stay unwashed for weeks, students
of the bodies of chocolate pre-pubescent girls –
and lock them in a house loaded
with cameras and microphones. Force them
to speak our language. Offer them a budget
scarcely adequate for food or tools,
and present them with tasks: to construct
a sunrise, say, or to stay under water
for an hour. Insert moles, temptresses, syphilis,
critics; divide them into bedrooms of three;
command the sun to scream overhead daily.
Scrutinise them as they disintegrate
into bedlam or rally round leaders. Then
make them stand up and nominate each other
for execution. (Naturally, the decision
on who survives the vote rests solely
with us.) Repeat the process occasionally
until only one remains – to be declared
The Greatest Impressionist of All Time –
before he, too, is brought before the guillotine.

World's Fair
Garry Winogrand

It might have been happening any time, anywhere, but of course
it's right it was happening in New York in 1964. The grassy area is
flat – primed for a fresh start – and the world's flags (the world as
understood in 1964) graze the frame of the picture in freeform
haze. What do background noises mean when the bench fizzes
with such music? Look at the legs, for instance, slanting this way
or that, crossed at the knees to focus each figure into a concise
form. The exception is a woman in their midst receiving touches of
comfort: in her distress she has suspended definition: feet slumped
on concrete as if dismembered from the body. A friend expressing
her concern has in turn intriguing things whispered to her.
Possibility takes over the tableau. The old man on the rightmost
end (the culmination, you might say, of a single figure sliding
ghostlike along) carries on in his newspaper-reading pose,
confident – look at that breaking outline of a smirk! – he still has a
role in this sensual frenzy. All the world's young in New York in
1964.

Search Engine

Start typing "Athens"
into your search engine

and predictively
you'll be sent to Athens,

Georgia. But isn't
the capital of Georgia

Tbilisi, you ask.
Home is neither here nor there.

You'd better think again
if you expect to find

the English northwest
when you enter "Manchester".

XXXXX

Dear Christodoulos,

Thank you for your letter and for your interest in being published by xxxxx. Of course I remember our session in xxxxx.

I have not started to read your submission. We may have a problem – as you'll see from our notes we can only (at this time at least) consider work by Irish authors. I hope this will change – but I need to ask you to clarify/confirm your nationality. I look forward to hearing from you.

Best wishes,

Sincerely,

xxxxx

Territorial

Your plate and your fork,
your cup and teaspoon are

your territory,
a warm press

you inhabit for forty years
more or less. Family

by proxy, then,
homely smells, a foetal curl.

Entitlement to shrinking
space, control.

Better off, you contend, than those
who move from pillar

to alien
outpost, borrowing

mugs as and when –
non-citizens

with no authorized
entry code or a healthcare

plan, constantly dodging
security.

Heaney after Rauschenberg

snug when into look down till rump away boot knee tall tops edge
deep that cool just like more turf than once milk with then fell
away sods over down down good turf cold slap peat curt cuts edge
head like them with

year flax down huge sods wove were best warm that grew like here
fill home wait dots into miss tell frog frog laid eggs this tell they
were rain then when were rank with that with bass down were sods
like some slap plop were some like were knew that hand

corn like grit dark were just from slit high each door when zinc
like oven edge when went then felt your fast into yard into when
bats were wing over eyes from dark like when shot shun fear like
rats

took path past over well away from road that down path cold bank
arcs then with care back ears down tail that took used when grey
yard this cold pipe then

late rain full week just clot hard knot that like wine upon lust then
ones that sent with cans full been with ones dark like eyes were
with byre when bath once bush turn sour felt like fair that each
year keep knew they

four that cool when with busy wood then came four into like deal
wood took turn that arms were with milk gold they then curd rich
that they wide like bowl long mine were wall soft with ease full
deal milk slap

when them into soft paws like tiny soon they were pump sure them
said like they till them dead days hung yard turn dung them fear
came back when rats shot with when pups just pups talk cuts town
they have kept down

with like full sail wing sock over with team back into land wake
fell rode back plod grow ever farm will away

jaws puff dead eyes down look dead like hoop from whom long
fade must come down wall been been from skin rise fall into pens
held them wall then fair days this with back draw sell same when
were room like ring your door this take your

sick home hard blow baby pram when came hand tell they were
away held hand hers with next went into room time left four foot
four foot year

grey only from cows into like away iron gate into bank with from
snug rise dead eyes used soon this they cock from left hand came
came down this sake spat take your time more hole tree wild more
said into mare hill back like that were that time ones that back
when

dark fill dead cold like they line from some keep full tall soon back
fish load from surf bend turf fear make they like clay seed shot
seem they show good from bark feel root pits live live wild land
root died when lain days long clay with eyes died hard bird huts
guts from like were with hope like land pits into sore stop they flop
down take fill then cold

west mayo crew they from when with eyes like bone skin rose fell
like they kept with beef men's then poor make food they like dogs
that been hard when they with they were hope less next like dark
once port ship free tart from good swim sink with zeal were

from that held arms came with have them word dead till

them them bare cold beef some from hook that pull neck look just
poor skin with inky once with grey pass find with cold bare down

from like byre like seed hand like milk keep

deep like down from gets that over from flat like back cold

burn that halt suds goes over like into this long over with tons that
thus

juts like lips' vice that fist drop that kind only pint bang home like
with life work horn will sits used wife will door hall

melt blue with down cold blue take wing holy name thus each they
lace cool them

that home with nose face port Iona ease next feet

walk came with talk took walk dusk hung like that swan swam
hawk calm need each held hawk prey talk with both wait late hate
hawk with talk deep walk

lady with left hurt your time rode easy days they buck from your
need gone self

came from Aran Aran rush wide arms rock tide that with with soft
land land each drew from land full

love with till sods were muck deep sods wall that sods fall clay
mush rain love this keep ring

dark hems long grey road that bind bank sure goes look away fire
hang keep sky's calm feel lost jolt down this only

when they upon test make sure that slip busy this down when job's
done sure dear seem fear fall that have wall

sink rock roof them with good this with that lost when full know
what mean gale that fear that your that down when hits very like
tame just wind huge that fear

salt four they peel rock pare down rind note head full hard head
salt wind

when love they into blue like from holy lips then back head wing
sang like took best poem made true tone

will from clay till rock hone edge blue grey when rain like that
land fuzz bone pain that wild eyes fire this bare bald with till pyre
head

each song they numb love tune pose like town tale will sell pale
love edge

each desk with dust read will play five will said jive when them
each note tyre eyes that wide they have once pens busy mime free
word with lost then taut they trip fall

they keep from with dark drop dank moss with rich when down
rope deep like when long from soft face over gave back your call
with tall into into some

Chances Are

```
<a class="twitter-timeline" href="https://twitter.com/search?
q=chance" data-widget-id="431483049818087424">Tweets about
"chance"</a>
<script>!function(d,s,id){var js,fjs=d.getElementsByTagName(s)
[0],p=/^http:/.test(d.location)?'http':'https';if(!
d.getElementById(id)){js=d.createElement(s);js.id=id;js.src=p+"://
platform.twitter.com/
widgets.js";fjs.parentNode.insertBefore(js,fjs);}}
(document,"script","twitter-wjs");</script>
```

Mayday

1

Ordinary: the word justifies plenty.
Just safeguarding the liberty of ordinary people.
No excessive force was employed,
they pre-empt accusations.
For scattering the anarchic element,
for defending the choices
of law-abiding citizens,
the police force is praised.
For its robust handling of the riots.
There are images of broken windows, outrage
at the loss of business.
The news at ten. The nine
o'clock news. Online media reports.

2

I fear she's right: it's no use risking
the smashing of our skulls.
That's enough, she says, we've had
our fun, made our mark,
have a point of view. Her stance
pulls me back, just. Rage shoots up
through the spine and straight to the head.
Molotov cocktails, face masks.
Body armour, the batons are out.
This operation was intended to immobilise troublemakers?
Rumblings of battle
drift from the high street. Our clothes are fuzzy
with anger, and wet.

3

The sky starts to weigh in with rain.
How many hours has it been?
A woman is sick. A man faints.
Clubs are raised above our heads.

Few try to fight. See how they like it
when we piss on them, someone yells.
The packed lunches are gone; we are forced
to ration the contents of our flasks.
It's soon evident we are the prisoners.
Hemmed in, picked out
of the campfire and put into a kettle.
Who's out to harm us? Who are we
being protected from? The cordon is impregnable.

4

They throw open their arms, lead us
to a side street. Guardians of order and law
greet us with shields and helmets.
Our communal compass points west.
We exchange hugs. Unwrap sweets and swap.
Indulge in the odd kiss.
Buoyed by horn-beeping we prance along.
Office workers wave from windows.
Stencil, graffiti, party whistles. There are fairies,
timpanists, cyclists, jugglers.
We share out packed lunches and flasks.
The new colours of May match our morning mood.
Today the streets belong to all.

Measures for the Prevention of Crime

I soak embryos in formaldehyde,
install them on the mantelpiece.
I keep them under surveillance –

but when the red eye shuts
they come alive and dance
like fuzzy torches in the dark,

rearrange my furniture,
raid my kitchen,
copulate in my swimming pool,

sneak into my bed.

Sincerely

Friendly, polite,
I have years of experience at home and abroad.
I'm looking for a job in your office/factory/shop
(preferably full-time).
I'm a good listener, well-educated,
I relish working in teams,
and I wish to build on my language and communication skills.

I thrive/crack under pressure
and love/hate working to targets.

I like books, music, movies or sports.
I enjoy socialising:
I have an extensive community of friends
on most reputable networking sites.
I get loads of invites and likes.
I've travelled a lot
and met many travellers from my country
(you can read all about it/see the pictures on my blog).

I'm a Gemini.
My favourite colour is red/blue.

I'm eager to learn, desperate
to buy into the ethos of your company.
I'm available whenever you text/email/message/call.
I await your reply with due anxiety.

Safe as Houses

1 Language

Language tells all.
It's as close to a god as we'll ever get.

Investigate it, believe it.

It lives in the earth and in our bones.
Its roots are in mortality.

2 Ship of Fools: The Luck of the Irish

A chara, –

They say our homes, shacks not many years before, went up in price more spectacularly than anywhere else in the world. That we built them anywhere as if there was no tomorrow. That we traded them like cards. We allowed the encroachment of funds that had no legs and re-zoned our practices to benefit those who could get their hands on the bulk of it. And to hell with the vulnerable. It's always been our patriotic duty to shield and venerate our loveable rogues; we are first rate at turning a blind eye and operating on mutual obligations; we thrive on secrecy, winks and nods, impenetrable language: our skills were honed over centuries of colonial rule (yes, we could carry on owing our former masters everything). We are being dubbed 'The Wild West of Europe' and 'As Haphazard as Kabul'. Yet, for a moment, there was a chance to set high standards of fairness and embark on pioneering campaigns to meet them. But our ship is full of fools and we blew it. Now they say we are sinking faster than anywhere else in the world, being washed away by a torrent of funds that never existed. Our homes are worth as much as the shacks our parents and grandparents toiled in. They say our luck has run out. That our only chance is charity. And that charity begins at home.

– Is mise,

3 The Architecture of Chance

- Engineer the falling into your hands of an arbitrary envelope.
- Watch out for cameras and men in uniform.
- Sneak it home, open and examine it.
- Argue its insignificance to yourself.
- Look at it intermittently, letting dust settle and cobwebs form on it, until it appears, illuminated, in your sleep.
- Probe the sender's name and address.
- Investigate their workplace and activity patterns.
- Unearth pictures of them.
- Compose a message and decide on a means of conveyance.
- Send.
- Don't bank on a response.
- Repeat the process, plotting co-ordinates towards construction as you go along.

4 Collected Emails

24 June 2008
I have only now received your email – I hadn't checked that account in ages! Yes, I'm still in Ireland. This is my work address, please contact me again if you wish. I wonder if I can still help you and how?

27 June 2008
Of course I will meet you. This all sounds very interesting. Let's arrange something maybe in two weeks' time. My parents are visiting at the moment.

5 August 2008
Sounds great, I will do my best to be there, it's in my diary now!

12 August 2008
Looking forward to seeing you.

9 October 2008
Just wondering how you are and if you are back in the country? I was in Poland for a week but now I'm back in the office.

26 November 2008
I'm afraid I won't be able to come this Thursday... a good friend of mine is leaving to work in Bahrain. The situation is getting complicated everywhere, even in my company, and more and more people are forced to join offices in Dubai, Bahrain and Qatar... I hope it won't happen to me because I really like Ireland.

3 March 2009
I have enjoyed the Christmas break and now I'm looking forward to my break in April. Still doing well in my job luckily, a lot of people lost their jobs in recent months.

19 March 2009
Today we learned our department is closing and we will be made redundant – on the 16th of April – getting closer every day!

I guess this adds another chapter to the whole architecture story!

Everything has come to a standstill in Ireland. I am hoping to stay for another while though – there is still a lot I want to see – the Cliffs of Moher, Giant's Causeway, Lakes of Killarney… there was never enough time for this. Then hunting for a job again!

23 March 2009
Unfortunately I won't be able to come… I'm finishing jobs in the office and as part of that I am flying to Cork. But I'm up for anything after the 16th of April!

18 May 2009
Kerry was wonderful, also a really nice sunny weekend. Was it the last one this summer? Looks like it… Yes, I am still doing a few days here and there. It looks like it's going to be very difficult to find a job, not to mention that with a foreign name it's twice as hard! I have been looking for nearly a month now. My boyfriend is still in the same company but not for long, I'd say… We'll look for a new destination soon.

When do you think this recession is going to end? I'm glad it doesn't affect poetry!

14 July 2009
We have moved apartments recently, I'm still trying to get internet connection there and I'm also getting a laptop this week. Everything's up in the air! We are in Ireland till Christmas. I have already started to look for work in the UK and I have interviews coming up. It's really bad for jobs over here so no point waiting any longer.

16 October 2009
I have moved to Scotland, I live in Glasgow now and work in the public sector. At work at the moment actually!

19 December 2009
Glasgow is fine, getting used to it, however I can't deny I miss Dublin…

The Group
Rilke

Chance orders faces like someone
arranging a hasty bouquet: by turns
it loosens them up and forces them dense,
joins two far apart, swaps this for that,
ignores one in the hub and blows another fresh,
throws a hound out of the mix like weed;
through muddled stalks and leaves it pulls
those which seem low up by their heads
and ties them, quite small, at the edge;
then stretches again, alters, removes, adjusts,
and has just time (for a last glance)
to skip back to the centre of the mat –
where the very next moment a slick weight-
swinger will flaunt his own weight.

Live the Life
Jean-Luc Godard

When the city lights go up the poet's endless beat begins.

He trades on his words
to build a sound clientele and establish
favourable conditions. Although charm
and strategy can be important factors in his career,
they are not necessary; but they do attract
the attention of patrons since they can be
immense sources of status.

With his dress, attitude and parlance
the poet indicates his trade.

Sometimes, in defiance of the rules,
he appeals directly to the reader. He charges
30 to 15,000 for a poem ranging from a few lines
to a series of pages; the rate
for a book varies between 5,000 and 50,000.

Lower grade poets average five to eight
readers a year. They make 4,000 to 8,000,
but others earn extraordinary sums: sixty
readers a week is not unknown during festival seasons.

A daily tax has been worked out.
In the English-speaking world 20,000 to 30,000 a week.
Payable annually.

Poets are subject to critical supervision.

Editors conduct raids, interrogations,
and anyone found infringing the law is sent
for publishability tests.

Controls have been attempted
on their movements: regulations forbid loitering with intent
at certain hours and in neighbourhoods
such as Soho or The Champs Elysées,
even though a sober poet is a liability, undesirable
because he doesn't stir up a fuss.

People imagine poets are perpetually inspired.
This is not true.
They do try to avoid blocks, by chemical or other means,
but when blocks are confirmed
suicide is rare.

The poet must always be at the reader's disposal;
he must accept anyone who pays.

Time off is allowed
after each profitability check. The poet
usually takes a trip, often
to see his family in the country.
Afterwards
he goes to the cinema or the seaside.

Let It Play: An Improvisation

Peter Michael Hamel

smell the baby's milkwhite breath freshening the air
    the panel blue as an Antipodean winter
        her nipple pierces the water's surface

a bird's song infiltrates the patter and glint of the piano
    the composer leaps and crashes
        stands still, listening

where has the teacher's fervour gone –
    dissipated over time, through battles against his horizons
        maybe with mechanisation

how do you return from flatness –
    a sharp shift will knock plate into plate
        new colours and sound suggest the words

reach into the consciousness of the child
    just before the transition
        spell unsayable things

14 March 2005

take the word butterfly

fly butter

by flutter

let by turf

fluttery B

bet fly rut

belfry tut

fry let tub

lefty burt

tuft Beryl

flery butt

yurt felt b

BT tel fury

bly Tufter

yule ft bet

butly fret

furl te byt

tyre t bluf

tryft lube

true t blyf

Jabez Clegg

The crawl here seems longer than it used to be. Things used to seem smaller than they used to be.

Your old friends are fuck knows where and how much notice should you give for a reunion?

In the mirror your belly sags a little and the hairs around your crotch are finally a designated forest.

When you're nine and your dad goes away you spill all over the place.

Doesn't matter if it's across a small sea or half way round the world, whether it's for a night only or eleven months.

You begin to curse: nine is the watershed.

In hotel rooms an empty bed is trigger.

When nostalgia is duller than it used to be you're doing alright.

This is dull.

It takes more than a quick nap to detox you of cumulative fatigue.

The streets are livelier and deader at the same time, differently.

Mediterranean cafe culture has infiltrated the red brick curry mile: milkshake mashed with shawarma and ristretto.

Satellites import music videos and political debate fronted by women and men, respectively.

A kaleidoscope of glitz and kitsch and cliché.

For all the new amenities you wouldn't trade your prime time here (except perhaps your personal brand of naivety).

These streets you own cooperatively with many before you and since. These placenames they mean so much and nothing. You didn't understand them then, you don't understand them now, differently.

These smells they smell of home. You carry it around.

Change is less welcome round here, suffusing the region with a grounding that's misleading. A grounding nonetheless.

The sense of place is strong. Which is at first cute, then pathetic.

Genius or Not

Saturday 6 February 2010: The Bunker

We leave our bags and anoraks at the door.
Inside we take our vests off and bare our prejudices
without having to listen. We turn the volume up
to a hundred. Stoke the passions. We are a partisan
lot, like it or lump it. We circulate coupons
and red tops, booze and tasteless jokes. Gays and blacks
are not welcome here; foreigners only if they're real
workingmen and have proved it for at least
ten years. We operate like wiseguys out of *Goodfellas*,
on favours and obligations. We remember
our dead with darts tournaments, retire
stools in their names. We can sell
whatever we want, smoke if we fancy it, and to hell
with Europe. We are standing our ground
in the face of all these invasions, taking refuge
in our multi-screen bunker until word's out
that dinner's on the table. Or till the cows
come home. Whichever's the latest.

Friday 16 April 2010: Vista

If you ignore the shimmering bulk on top you can get a measure of
the jumble below. The naked trees and assorted pylons and wires.
The untreated buildings with bright green window frames. The
magnolia-cream, chocolate-brown, deep sea-blue and just-grey
facades of a terrace. Revolving advertisements for sundry
businesses in the estate agent's window. The butcher's and the
solicitor's. Trimmed hedges and dogs in small gardens. Clothes
lines. At eye level a phalanx of aerials turned northwards or
eastwards, a spire, rooftiles crooked or broken and sooty-black, a
shining white statue of Jesus. Are these seagulls you can hear or
police sirens? Is the drill bursting old pavements or force-entering
a home? You're standing on cigarette butts and flowers. Birdshit
on the parapet feels like splashes of yellow paint. Coffee lingers on
your tongue, there's a whiff of ash in your nostrils.

Wednesday 25 August 2010: On the Road

This is tricky, dangerous – almost certainly
illegal – on the potholed roads of north Fingal.
Eternal roadworks – while a stretch
is being fixed another's cut up by nothing more than

rain. Machinery, construction altering
the shore – how long will that brand new house
stand before erosion collapses it
to the sea? The spot where we crashed

that day – helicopter, tailbacks, ambulance,
baby seat on the asphalt, that unidentified
man. Off the beaten lanes, through a relic
of a town neat as a 1950s experiment,

into deep country. Golf course. GAA.
Harvesters and tractors. Slow crop transport.
More potholes – and cowdung.
Horseriding on the roads. Killer

bends. The town with both a north
and a south beach, *infested*
with commuters and a Polish shop on every
corner. Old townfolk too. A motor yard.

Monday 11 October 2010: The Wanderings of Sebald

a full hour
empty of doings and undoings
is rare –

I consider my pace,
slow the beat in my head
so that sweat beads don't start trickling down my back

or spread to perfume my underarms –
I throw my jacket off,
breathe estuary air,

sit on the roadside with the book
of the wanderings of Sebald
open –

would it be classed as fiction (823 or simply F),
German literature (833),
European travel (914), historical geography (911), memoir
(920Seb),

poetry (821 or 831) perhaps –
it has claims on philosophy too,
photography, art, history – time studies –

the air cools my body,
how many more has it cooled
in its time

Saturday 13 November 2010: Airport

When I'm in airports I think about death.
Especially if I'm travelling alone.
That's predictable enough. My son
cried last night because he wanted
to come along. It's dawn
and we throw food down our throats,
build ourselves up to carry on. I yawn
and spill coffee all over the table. The gloves
are off. Boots and belt too.
It doesn't matter about your babyface, precious,
or your toned pushed-up body,
get lumped on board
along with the lot of us. We are more
than just meat. We are more than just
meat. We are more than
just meat. Plastic and steel. Machines
that miraculously stay up. If you stop to think
what might go wrong
you'll only freeze. Have faith
the inconceivable clinical snuffing out will be delayed
or cancelled.

Wednesday 19 January 2011: Lines for Cézanne's 172nd Birthday

A cleaned out white plate,
its perimeter centrifugal blocks of primary colours.
A fork and a knife at an angle encompassing a scrunched-up
    napkin.
A plastic Coca-Cola bottle
removed twice its own height
from the glass into which its contents have been poured,
fizzing and eating up ice cubes.
A mobile phone, flat and idle.
Folded dinner menus,
salt and pepper pots,
sugar bowls (white and brown),
sachets of tomato ketchup, tartare sauce, English mustard, vinegar,
    brown sauce –
vertical and tidy at the corner
opposite a shut copy of the latest Muldoon
and a sponsored pen feverishly writing.
All on a square black table.

Wednesday 23 February 2011: Full Circle

River runs into itself, washes into land
– slack undertow –
sand, grass, asphalt, bricks.
Doctored photographs, signatures, CGI on the streets:
oil portraits smudged.
Howling wind.
Sunrays like rain aslant through clouds endlessly hovering.
Tiny light creeps out of night –
a thief loitering all day, shadowing.
Dusk falls silent.
Blinds won't keep beams from screens.
Murmuring, drinking, muffled sex, toilet rests.
Come the dawn the pattering of feet, watches being set.
Off out on the train, the bus, the tram –
a lift breaks down.
OUT OF ORDER.
Management's at fault.
Battle lines being drawn – membranous, permeable –
a drone of complaints dampening critical patch.
Celebrations aborted, desire doused.
The revolution botched.

From Something to Nothing
Francis Alÿs

The International Monetary Fund (IMF) is an organization of 187 countries, working to foster global monetary cooperation, secure financial stability, facilitate international trade, promote high employment and sustainable economic growth, and reduce poverty around the world.

Το Διεθνές Νομισματικό Ταμείο (ΔΝΤ) είναι μια οργάνωση από 187 χώρες, που εργάζονται για την προώθηση της παγκόσμιας νομισματικής συνεργασίας, να εξασφαλιστεί η οικονομική σταθερότητα, η διευκόλυνση του διεθνούς εμπορίου, την προώθηση της υψηλής απασχόλησης και της βιώσιμης οικονομικής ανάπτυξης, και τη μείωση της φτώχειας σε όλο τον κόσμο.

Le Fonds monétaire international (FMI) est une organisation de 187 pays, travaillent à promouvoir la coopération monétaire mondiale, assurer la stabilité financière, de faciliter le commerce international, de promouvoir l'emploi élevé et une croissance économique durable et la réduction pauvreté dans le monde.

O Fundo Monetário Internacional (FMI) é uma organização de 187 países, trabalhando para promover a cooperação monetária internacional, a estabilidade financeira segura, facilitar o comércio internacional, promover o emprego de alta e crescimento econômico sustentável e reduzir a pobreza mundo.

Is é an Ciste Airgeadaíochta Idirnáisiúnta (CAI) eagraíocht de 187 tír, ag obair chun comhoibriú idirnáisiúnta airgeadaíochta, cobhsaíocht airgeadais a áirithiú, trádáil idirnáisiúnta a éascú, fostaíocht ard agus fás eacnamaíoch inbhuanaithe a chur chun cinn agus ar fud an domhain bochtaineacht a laghdú.

Der Internationale Währungsfonds (IWF) Organisation von 187 Ländern vertreten und arbeiten für internationale Zusammenarbeit, die finanzielle Stabilität zu gewährleisten, den internationalen Handel erleichtern, ein hohes Beschäftigungsniveau und nachhaltiges Wirtschaftswachstum Förderung und weltweite Armut.

Representado por el Fondo Monetario Internacional (FMI) la organización de 187 países y el trabajo de cooperación internacional para asegurar la estabilidad financiera, facilitar el comercio internacional, alto nivel de empleo y la promoción de un crecimiento económico sostenible y la pobreza en el mundo.

Represented by the International Monetary Fund (IMF) organization of 187 countries and work for international cooperation to ensure financial stability, facilitate international trade, high employment and the promotion of sustainable economic growth and poverty in the world.

Εκπροσωπείται από το Διεθνές Νομισματικό Ταμείο (ΔΝΤ) την οργάνωση από 187 χώρες και να εργαστούν για τη διεθνή συνεργασία για την εξασφάλιση της χρηματοοικονομικής σταθερότητας, τη διευκόλυνση του διεθνούς εμπορίου, υψηλής απασχόλησης και την προώθηση της βιώσιμης οικονομικής ανάπτυξης και της φτώχειας στον κόσμο.

Représentée par le Fonds monétaire international (FMI) l'organisation de 187 pays et travailler pour la coopération internationale pour assurer la stabilité financière, de faciliter le commerce international, d'emploi élevé et une croissance économique durable et la pauvreté dans le monde.

Representados pelo Fundo Monetário Internacional (FMI) organização de 187 países e trabalhar para a cooperação internacional para assegurar a estabilidade financeira, facilitar o comércio internacional, o emprego de alta e crescimento econômico sustentável ea pobreza no mundo.

Léirithe ag an Ciste Airgeadaíochta Idirnáisiúnta (CAI) a eagrú 187 tíortha agus obair um chomhar idirnáisiúnta ar a chinntiú cobhsaíocht airgeadais, trádáil idirnáisiúnta a éascú, fostaíocht ard agus fás eacnamaíoch inbhuanaithe agus bochtaineachta ar fud an domhain.

Produziert vom Internationalen Währungsfonds (IWF) um 187 Ländern und arbeiten für internationale Zusammenarbeit, um finanzielle Stabilität zu gewährleisten organisieren, den internationalen Handel erleichtern, ein hohes Beschäftigungsniveau und ein nachhaltiges Wirtschaftswachstum und Armut in der Welt.

Producido por el Fondo Monetario Internacional (FMI) para 187 países y el trabajo para la cooperación internacional para organizar a asegurar la estabilidad financiera, facilitar el comercio internacional, alto nivel de empleo y el crecimiento económico sostenible y la pobreza en el mundo.

Produced by the International Monetary Fund (IMF) for 187 countries and work to organize international cooperation to ensure financial stability, facilitate international trade, high employment and sustainable economic growth and poverty in the world.

Producido por el Fondo Monetario Internacional (FMI) para 187 países y el trabajo de organizar la cooperación internacional para asegurar la estabilidad financiera, facilitar el comercio internacional, alto nivel de empleo y el crecimiento económico sostenible y la pobreza en el mundo.

Produziert vom Internationalen Währungsfonds (IWF) für 187 Länder und die Arbeit der Organisation der internationalen Zusammenarbeit, um finanzielle Stabilität zu gewährleisten, den internationalen Handel erleichtern, ein hohes Beschäftigungsniveau und ein nachhaltiges Wirtschaftswachstum und Armut in der Welt.

Léirithe ag an Ciste Airgeadaíochta Idirnáisiúnta (CAI) le haghaidh 187 tíortha agus le hobair na heagraíochta an chomhair idirnáisiúnta, chun a chinntiú cobhsaíocht airgeadais, trádáil idirnáisiúnta a éascú, fostaíocht ard agus fás eacnamaíoch inbhuanaithe agus bochtaineachta ar fud an domhain.

Produzido pelo Fundo Monetário Internacional (FMI) para 187 países eo trabalho da cooperação internacional, para garantir a estabilidade financeira, facilitar o comércio internacional, o emprego de alta e crescimento econômico sustentável e pobreza no mundo.

Produit par le Fonds monétaire international (FMI) pour 187 pays et le travail de coopération internationale, pour assurer la stabilité financière, de faciliter le commerce international, d'emploi élevé et une croissance économique durable et la pauvreté dans le monde.

Παράγεται από το Διεθνές Νομισματικό Ταμείο (ΔΝΤ) για 187 χώρες και το έργο της διεθνούς συνεργασίας, για την εξασφάλιση της χρηματοοικονομικής σταθερότητας, τη διευκόλυνση του διεθνούς εμπορίου, υψηλής απασχόλησης και της βιώσιμης οικονομικής ανάπτυξης και της φτώχειας στον κόσμο.

Produced by the International Monetary Fund (IMF) for 187 countries and the project of international cooperation, to ensure financial stability, facilitate international trade, high employment and sustainable economic growth and poverty in the world.

Producido por el Fondo Monetario Internacional (FMI) para 187 países y el proyecto de cooperación internacional, para asegurar la estabilidad financiera, facilitar el comercio internacional, alto nivel de empleo y el crecimiento económico sostenible y la pobreza en el mundo.

Produziert vom Internationalen Währungsfonds (IWF) für 187 Länder und die internationale Kooperation, um finanzielle Stabilität zu gewährleisten, den internationalen Handel erleichtern, ein hohes Beschäftigungsniveau und ein nachhaltiges Wirtschaftswachstum und Armut in der Welt.

Léirithe ag an Ciste Airgeadaíochta Idirnáisiúnta (CAI) le haghaidh 187 tíortha agus comhoibriú idirnáisiúnta, chun a chinntiú cobhsaíocht airgeadais, trádáil idirnáisiúnta a éascú, fostaíocht ard agus fás eacnamaíoch inbhuanaithe agus bochtaineachta ar fud an domhain.

Produzido pelo Fundo Monetário Internacional (FMI) para 187 países e da cooperação internacional, para garantir a estabilidade financeira, facilitar o comércio internacional, o emprego de alta e crescimento econômico sustentável e pobreza no mundo.

Produit par le Fonds monétaire international (FMI) pour 187 pays et la coopération internationale, pour assurer la stabilité financière, de faciliter le commerce international, d'emploi élevé et une croissance économique durable et la pauvreté dans le monde.

Παράγεται από το Διεθνές Νομισματικό Ταμείο (ΔΝΤ) για 187 χώρες και τη διεθνή συνεργασία, για την εξασφάλιση της χρηματοοικονομικής σταθερότητας, τη διευκόλυνση του διεθνούς εμπορίου, υψηλής απασχόλησης και της βιώσιμης οικονομικής ανάπτυξης και της φτώχειας στον κόσμο.

Produced by the International Monetary Fund (IMF) for 187 countries and international cooperation, to ensure financial stability, facilitate international trade, high employment and sustainable economic growth and poverty in the world.

University

To live off the fat
of the land, a well-kept

secret. Rubbish
mountains pile up

swept off expanding
village girths, continuous

cities. To build with
half-tiles, broken glass,

rusting out of
joint iron, flaking

wooden slats. To eat out
of tins, fruit skins, luxurious

waste. To scale
the heights, to live off skills

and words worth
their weight in gold.

A 21st Century Portrait

Douglas Gordon & Philippe Parreno

His poise
begins to disintegrate before our obsessive eyes,
tracked by seventeen cameras.
Sweat starts suddenly to soak his shirt
and we are left nonplussed.

A mercenary, frame by frame
he edges away from our sympathy
towards a self-generated cauldron.
Everything mists up.
Suppressed by a wall of noise
he is irretrievable; the passions descend,
they consume him

away from our vulturine apprehension
into a place neither here nor there,
while we watch him
all the while watching us,
making no apparent headway.

Adventures in Dentistry

David Lynch was at one time fascinated with dentistry.
Reportedly. Allegedly. With extreme procedures and mouths
        distended
beyond recognition. With the inerasable

memory of foul odours. Pictures of decaying gums. Hereabouts
The Dentist is feared, hated and revered in equal measure
by the inhabitants of Gangland, a territory decent people won't
        venture to

except behind TV sets or tabloids. A foreign country.
You couldn't speak the interrogation practices therein [*too
        unpleasant*
to record, certainly too grim to versify

*on paper in good old-fashioned ink – though if I try typing directly
        onto history-less*
screen they might be more forthcoming]. There are rumours
of guns held behind counters. Shutters down indicates

heavies are ready to take the first hit in a bullet storm. Quicken
        your pace
just in case an ambush is imminent, and be mindful
who you might be funding with your penchant for cappuccinos

[*should I even be sharing this?*] Perhaps you'd better stick
to reformatting timeless classics and Old Masters or at most
        sanctioned distortions
of them: refer, for example, to Francis Bacon's screaming

popes with their dark ulcerous mouths
appropriated from medical journals. You won't likely cause bother
        then,
little or no risk of injury to your anaesthetised

jaw or like some unwitting dummy having your cheek pierced for sheer torture. Have you noticed how many devices early Michael Haneke borrows from Lynch?

Consequences

Drivers busy crossing themselves when passing churches
have caused accidents,
        fatalities even. I've seen it,
local pedestrians know it. Ring round the hospitals
to ascertain which is the least chaotic. An operation costs
an arm and a leg. This is no joke! If it was a joke
I'd have clearly signposted it – otherwise I deserve all the grief
I get. Our respective countries have gone
to the dogs, they're salvageable by nothing (©Harry Clynn).
Place your bets
        or hurry along. Yes, things have changed,
but I'm pretty sure my hometown hasn't moved
to the coast. Some people (meaning men) grab their testicles there
whenever they spy a priest. There really is
a George Bush Centre for Intelligence.
CIA: WTF?
        DIY education can land you
in heavy arrears. If words are louder than actions
let's see your thunderclap. Careful, though, what you express
and how you express it, it might earn you
a prison sentence. In light of this
        can you analyse
BEE's Twitter rant? Discuss, further, the similarities (meaning
differences) between DFW's Captain Video and MBW (Mr
        Brainwash
for long) in *Exit Through The Gift Shop* as paradigms
of a desire for an endless present
and a fear of mortality. Just because they stop
whispering when you enter the room
        doesn't mean you're not
paranoid. If they pussyfoot around you be sure it is they
who are in turmoil. Someday I'll write that thesis
on how we're happy to have stopped experiencing things as long
as we're able to record, document and hence
prove we've experienced them. Photography: take
note. Please, let's consign that 'we' business to the dustbin
of nationhood. By the way,
        what does pronouncing asterisk as "asterix",

sixth as "sick-th", or ask as "axe", or even the wanton articulation
of "r" sounds where none are marked, say about your
racioethnosocioeducational status
or allegiances?

Sales Pitch (Issue 3113)

Twelve years on from Titanic
Winslet and Di Caprio are reunited.
Naturally, they make our cover.

> *a shattered hand*
> *curiously prominent*
> *face up*
> *trunk contorted*

In our culture pages, Springsteen performs for Barack Obama,
who is profiled further in
in expectation of his inauguration.

> *as if in ecstasy*
> *a foot*
> *at an impossible angle*
> *back against a doorframe*

We report, among others, on Julia Roberts kissing a man,
Rachida Dati at work days after giving birth
and Jean-Paul Belmondo (75) with Barbara (33).

> *heavy beneath another*
> *his mouth & eyes half shut*
> *she looks out*
> *fists clenched*

The spectacle of war
(shocking and utterly unimaginable)
puts a skewer through the day's concerns.

> *caught in an attempt to scream*
> *rags blood debris*
> *punctuate the composition*
> *the narrative frozen*

We also have film star babies, credit crunch suicides,
a gallery of portraits of Charlotte Rampling
and various puzzles – solvable even by beginners.

> *a new icon*
> *face strained*
> *eyebrows raised*
> *eyes fixed somewhere dim*

As always, our production values are marvellous,
the colours brilliant, the feel opulent and glossy.
We provide a window to the world.

Four Manifestos

1

A red rose
sends fragrance to rise
from my immaculate shirt.
Sunshine, delectable fare, exotic teas,
refine my mind.

2

Watching him
it's as if I need local fact and links
or state sponsorship
to speak.
Rather, my words
roam; they find audience
in time.

3

We too have to eat
and shit, apply for credit
and promote ourselves
for a fuck. We get our kicks
from drink and trade,
gambling and cars.

4

I spill out of myself.
My body sags
and smells. I wipe their children's mess
off the kitchen floor.
I'm occupied
with what occupies me.

Two Nudes

r.

She sleeps.
She is ethereal, escapes
from photographs
in filmy layers. A wisp
swathed in snow. The cold does not faze her, she
commands it. Water,
she craves it. She pervades it.
Watch it become ice, slumber
through time.

s.

Her hair is jet-black and pulled
back so tight her eyes arc
skywards. Her skin is taut and livid and
sparkles like wine. She is
streetwise. Her mouth is foul and her mind scythes
through jobs. She has energy
to burn. She storms
out of her clothes as if her bustling
presence can't be checked.

**com
pass
ion**

I'm drawn west
wards, staggering unbalanced
as if my ear
's been hacked off. Tuned
out. I fall in a gutter, mud un
dried in the north
ern sun. The wine here
's corked. In time I'm hauled
out by a dark
hand, her flailing be
flowered hair conceal
ing a surgic
al mind. We lie and talk
of home. South is my orient
ation, I say. South
is where I repeated
ly come
from, she offers. Half
arcs there on the night sky
map our motions.

Dissolution

time   (continuous)
s t r e t c h e s   andcontracts
                or
is   measured   in   units
by laboratories
                        operating
with digitised particles
& compartmental
existence

when you've found a way
(the secret)
to exit   and enter
                                    at will
any temporal
                                    unavailability
                idleness
                        silence
is put down to
(interpreted through)
grave circumstance

molecules come together
(solid-physical-corporeal)
into matter
& disappearance
            into web space
suggests dissolution
            or an escape

(Iván Zulueta foreshadowed this with his film *Arrebato* in 1979 –
though it too had its antecedents: *L'invenzione di Morel*, a 1974
film by Emidio Greco, based on a 1940 novel by Adolfo Bioy
Casares, based in turn on HG Wells' 1896 *The Island of*

                    threads left
            untied
    no resolution   (blurred)

                    story   lines
          absurd
                        unfulfilled
              promises
                        & dispersed
   into
                  in   differ   ence

L'Homme au nez Cassé
Rodin

smoke stains
the image   a fading reproduction
              ashes blown
all over the floor

windows   wide   open

(sliding down
the cream wall   a bundle
        of unresolved

heavyboned
deadweight

drunk head of curly hair
         hard stubble
motormind   an even faster mouth
                        (keep up!)

knee joints   popping
                        out
pills spilled
all over engineering textbooks
         artist's materials
         astrophysics notes
         science magazines

ontological investigations might elucidate
         connections and nodes

the messy fucks and lewd exposures

eyes looking straight ahead
clearly
              s n o o k e r e d
cannot see the whole
         just the crescent

within the mass of contradictions
                    family vs family
                    child vs children
                    tongue vs language
                              & a woman
who may or may not
admit him
          (r e t a l i a t i o n
for failing to admit to her
                         by name)

the sea calls

those temporary sirens
wailing
with Baltic accents
                    dancing
          on tables   bopping
                              in clubs

backtracking to an idealised
beat
                    and he
beating a retreat
to repeated
treats

Palmists

In the car I expound my thesis (formed as I speak – a perpetual
present) on the daftness of fortunetelling. Let's assume (I begin)
there are those who see what's yet to occur. If our reason for
finding out is to change something undesirable, then the assumed
capability of foresight renders the exercise invalid, since (I reason)
if we could alter a predetermined course of events then it wouldn't
be pre-determined at all. And if we can't, then knowing what's
round the corner doesn't help – and it's not much fun at all.
Though I guess the last bit's subjective.

We bisect (a) wounded land. (The) children are sleeping in the
back exhausted by e(x)ternal tensions. For a moment we talk as if
we're unestranged. There's a neat fissure in time. We make love *en
plein air* for the first time. I'm persuaded to go skinny-dipping. We
discover we can unlearn. The wireless is stuck: it establishes a
continuum. Memory is an act of re-membering.

What is it they (can) tell? Something already understood? A route
out of (into) anxiety? Some vague energy? Extrapolation gleaned
from jewellery, accent, shoes? Sherlock Holmes is a figment. A
construct. Illusionists can convince audiences they possess
knowledge (powers) they couldn't possibly have access to, while
refuting claims of paranormal ability.

We may compile personalities through timeline logs, traces left
(virtually) by physical activity. Work backwards to determine
where (when) we began to unravel. We cover old ground while
time carries on – stretching everything beyond cognition. Or is
time cyclical? In an increased capacity to fit action into ever-
decreasing loops, memory becomes an act of (re)creation.

I drive in a perpetual present. The fissure is firmly shut. I bid to
escape to a few moments ago, into timelessness. Where (the)
words do not reach. To exist beyond the corner. To be able to
swerve round the body lying there.

Prime Time

over the corner brilliant take on the team like it what a gossip
tonight modern unlimited hold on mission pirates anytime
anywhere get watching one great website comprehensive
breakdown including too good to miss courtesy 24 hours .ie great
value travel insurance if i could give you a standing design body
shape turns more heads the best mirror i could try imagine myself
nonstop set up this plane trying to save from the makers of
candycrush new saga available in circus east west colourful world
boundaries vanish spirit downsize afford two tough people the
same role eh? any need let go nothing personal don't have to act
energy at home

choice music screens first time dedicates one anticipated hour
centre stage song of the year celebrating talent at a glance health
appears similar my needs different look fresh focus the care that
matters to private excellence family half scalpel first the bahamas
two weeks be so nice in a collision glass safety model simulation
advanced for entire fragile organs especially on the inside makes it
safer a car best your morning interject one moment analysis daily
funds lunchtime lives at drivetime risk radio here he comes up to
last shave night chest lads no way change wax man rest hunger
quarter beef crisp range serious ma

heavy downpours this country evening

simply new irresistible taste welcome late five fat acts eurovision
featuring boys composition man row finalist and emerging talent
tonight greatest area created guys social networks humans built
rights toilet toughest challenge getting home breathe nose escape
free magazine festival guide legends mail collection free bilingual
big read small price healthcare save february half price family
enjoy benefits insurer special there must end tv evening laptop
must end fish families feast succulent flavour fillets tongue-tastic
breadcrumbs choice multivitamins up energy difference helping
your active life last da other partner messing original starts hero
tom name diner so good at killing violence tonight coverage meet
nationwide

its long eve seachtan marta supporting area arts 51 inventions
created by these guys humans know my rights toughest challenge
get home breathe nose escape free daily festival inside beautiful
bits irish small choose family favourites dinner dish percent vegan
just fresh offers clear orthodontic removable discreet notice dentist
technology metal affordable price plan smile book discount march
great deal home insurance sorry worked out ladder offer

taste outdoor freedom land bike sea savour memories for years
discovery series only weekend times fresh fish fun families
fantastic fillets flavour feast delicious coated catch yr morning
briefing points made fatality analysis news lunchtime price
consumer catchup sentiment turn your radio on unlimited that's it
simple so what you waiting great offer stomping ground
underbelly now take on capital tracks

wakes up the fresher rise on its way the baker it's famous every
morning the best to you life cannot always choose what you do
who you are we are the every coffee i am the master captain of my
soul enchanting stories animation winning music orchestra in
concert enjoy stunning films performs live in energy on sale
comprehensive member from month when they're insured it's you
today let's go as irish as the land comes from here right traceable
to farms no buts always will be right now at least sofas limited
extra collections price also year's free credit

you can explore more each weekend tracks that premier feeling
your morning briefing how do you respond 14 new funds risk cries
of pain close catch up your sentiment day now you can experience
horizon extraordinary broadband faster than sky incredible six
more can you afford connection switch on the works theatre
highlights failure artist honoured and music luck in the world
contenders

conquer every day stag machine my brother invite him insane
seven no yeah time to roam free i could've sworn the emperor
keep alternating cinema charges include inspiration engineered
fastest brand revolution fabulously families natural donegal tasty
no no no grand epic jackpot guaranteed keeps rolling more prizes
and won't get you into his arms buy you love mum can all you
gotta do is coverage better across don't get our call message post
to network power god fewer news calories at anything guess my

day event name buy one get half you can mix and free range and
doctor organic is included well ok not kitchen conquer life orange

with seven restaurant no problem connect serve use reactivate skin
ability multi-action inspired technology looks for radiant number
one anti-aging who is that man upload your four special washing
must end amazing save lowest five hundred laptop enjoy real
martial cows half gold kill every set up nonstop something last
friend in the current series

now you can experience the extraordinary from faster phone
incredible for over six more can you afford free the inspiration
irelands revolution gathered in their masses witches and black
today dead greeks rise of an empire who is that talent i've been
waiting wait a second looking out you're not another year it's late
late news family violence man

tell five finalists catch me favourite song now something terrible
happened i made a promise this is sunday horizon clever box
recording things four programmes any exciting screen you might
like amazing channels delivered fibre unlimited bundle makers
together we can stop smoke one working floor key ask test to
check for you stub obvious cooking unattended plan your access
close doors at the ready together we can stop fire um yeah away on
holiday defo its rice new caramel let me take you hell freeze in
cinemas smallest break shoot it there goes our red line how you did
that no claims forgiveness redefining

and this evening right the country heavy

simply new cooking half taste i've been waiting whoa how it's
done you're not here another year it's late the break oh here we go
join the biggest names movie events that hollywood can't be just
one for the first virtuoso to conduct by wednesday tickets from
slash times are downsize two people role there's no need let you go
nothing by now you can experience incredible for six months more
can you afford switch there's a big change heads aerosols counts
less waste compress new smaller cams last just as long well give
money back green band are you fed up motivation is short
maintaining why you eat private consultations weight for life call
us today or visit presidency democracy is so overrated welcome

glitzy house and curly look together for the love restore granny's jigs proud eurosong heritage special flashing

hawaiian broadband i just know something terrible sometimes they turn up she leads her on heartache i can see why family is promise continuing the answers give your kids milk strong bones to absorb vitamin gives them all the heroes here he comes shine up to last night shave get this no way how come rest of us hunger deluxe man barbecue range serious friends going on about it seen it busy season one i know it doesn't matter amazing game walking wire daddy plenty where than came from latest shows better sky extreme deep swamp land breakfast menu served white sausage good luck cookie wholegrain good cereal collision bowl made of glass safety simulation entire body all impact fragile especially makes it safer best in the world all these years friends all on holiday seven and a half million one day to show shot comprehensive surely to avoid rubbish written off go to insurance the way little david morning everyone sprinkles covers us around for spread as irish as the land right here and right here irish no ifs 100% all the goodness full whole introducing super aspiring gruelling heat cooks beyond nerve-wracking twist plate proud sponsor stingray fairies

sky this is my life partner original comedy no way t-shirts you guys work i know what you gonna say great value car quote us or visit can you get this in blue freedom on land savour the memories get active starting with your walking guide this weekend i don't know thousands of people shaking their tv incredible in a bundle free for six months switch call three welcome aboard new york london every twenty minutes the best in cinemas national war play soft book softer combo world you win post if you're heading explore commission card safer than credit use it where you can see more inspiring praise city what car all new engineered fastest brand revolution now healthcare can save more under half price great value enjoy leading benefits we're there now have free shipping delivery value returns delivered unlimited

Morning

Ungaretti

sorethroat
fucksake

Why I live in Egypt

The lifestyle here is very simple. I start my day with coffee and fruit on the beach in the morning, and then either work on the beach talking to people about the diving courses, or take a group out and guide them through the coral. In the evenings the whole working community gathers to play pool, have a simple dinner, maybe of falafel or Egyptian pizza, and watch The Simpsons at 6 p.m. – some things are the same all over!

*

The lifestyle here is easily understood, uncomplicated and humble. My day starts on the beach in the company of coffee and fruit, and at that time I work talking to human beings about courses in plunging steeply downwards or disable groups and guide them so as to inspect all or part of the coral. In the evenings the extent of the functioning community gather to co-operate in pool, own simple dinner, maybe falafel or Egyptian pizza, and clock the Simpsons at 6 post mortem – some personal belongings are personal belongings all end!

*

The elegance of biography in this place is easily understood, straightforward and of low rank. A particular period of my past jumps on the edge of the sea in the commercial business of coffee and fruit, and at that period I campaign talking to human livings around routes in plunging exaggeratedly towards a lower point or put crops out of action and control them so as to examine all or the role of the coral. In the evenings the degree of the functioning society infer to co-operate in a common fund, own low intelligence dinner, maybe Arab pepper or Egyptian Italian pie, and clock the family at six post mortem – at least a small amount of private belongings are personal belongings any whatever end.

*

The elegance of my story at this time is understood easily, and it is also moving straight ahead. But I am of low rank. A certain period of my past leaps forth to the edge of the sea, to the business of coffee and fruit. During that period I campaigned to men in living through the route of thrusting quickly towards a point of lower levels to put related people out of action and control them. Thus I could examine everyone for the role of the chorus. At the conclusion the level of functioning in the society leads to co-operating into a low intelligence common fund to owning all, maybe Arab, Egyptian and Italian food. Clock the family at post mortem six – at least an amount of their belongings are belongings whatever the end.

*

The beauty of my story is now easy to see – advancing sharply even though I am of low worth. A certain period from my past leaps to the forefront of memories: the time I was in the businesses of coffee and fruit. Then I campaigned to men on surviving through the principle of pushing lower qualities to incapacitate and control brothers. In so doing I examined everyone for the role of collaborator. In the end the low level of activity and intelligence in society leads to my ownership of the common fund – perhaps Southern and Eastern thought too. Count the families, and at least after the sixth death an amount of their belongings becomes movable possession however they die.

Civilisation's Golden Dawn: A Slide Show

The navy and army sail the Mediterranean, invading areas as far north as Modern Russia.

Popular singer Yiannis Poulopoulos – open shirt, hairy chest – tickles a young girl.

In the 1830s a new language called katharévousa (meaning pure) was created.

Plaka. Molon Labe. Achilles. Zappeion.

Poustraki finished, you understand? Poustrakia run out. Come kolompichtes, soft ass actors, actresses e assholes ass. Look poutanaki comes your time. D Pull, pull, comes your time. D comes and your police guard the ass after your gamane you gamane the Pakistani man. Sisters torn. Albanian fucking asshole, fucking with Albanian asshole.

Man sitting on a ledge looking moody, stone mountains hanging mid-air behind him.

It's a presidential republic.

A Mazda car. A Carlsberg bag. Picnic on the grass.

Processions leave churches at midnight to re-enact the search for Christ's body.

Riding on the Athens Tram. Happy.

Crisis is a Greek word. Crisis means having people enter parliament who'll bring the country five hundred years back.

Stalagmites, stalactites, navigated by boat.

Albanian refugees are given shelter and jobs.

Feeding pigeons. Isthmus. Amusement park. Some ruins.

Popular singer Kostas Karalis on a personally signed promotional postcard.

The Ancient Greek phrase μολὼν λαβέ (molòn labé; reconstructed Ancient Greek pronunciation [mo'lɔːn la'be]; Modern Greek pronunciation [mo'lon la've]) means "Come and take them". It is a classical expression of defiance reportedly spoken by King Leonidas I in response to the Persian army's demand that the Spartans surrender their weapons at the Battle of Thermopylae. It is an exemplary use of a laconic phrase.

Churches. Monuments. Moving escalators.

The system of dowries is no longer practiced.

Boy poses alongside tsolias (meaning presidential guard).

Would you call a male politician throwing a glass of water and a right-left-right hook at female members of parliament on live TV macho, or funny?

The unknown soldier.

Laughing so hard she ends up in hospital.

Boy sitting on a ledge, stone mountains hanging mid-air behind him, looking down.

Food and hospitality are important to culture.

Thessaloniki: a goalkeeper lunge, an open window, broken glass, a deep cut above the left eye, to hospital for stitches.

All packed up.

City dwellers participate in exercise, go to parks and walk their dogs. In rural areas people visit each other and host parties.

Out of focus at proscenium of amphitheatre. Man tossing coin demonstrates unbelievable acoustics.

Literally: "number". The Huffington Post translates it as "circus act". My dictionary says "odd character". None is individually adequate.

At the border with Yugoslavia. Bird, nationality unknown, shits on boy's head. A lucky omen.

Who's this striking young couple?

Ochi (meaning No) Day celebrates pride.

Impressed by the large flower clock at Patras.

More ruins.

Folk dances range from the festive and happy to the serious and solemn.

Poystraki finish, got it? Run the poystrakia. ADE kwlompichtes, assholes, kwloy actors with actors of kwloy assholes. Look at poytanaki, your time is coming. Trava Trava, comes the time. PE and comes your police guard the kwlarakia after your your gamane gamane which Pakistanis eh. Xeskismenes sisters. Gamimenes Albanian kwlotrypides Albanian gamimenes, kwlotrypides.

Popular singer Stamatis Kokotas in a smart suit smiles for the camera.

Ascending the stairs to the airplane. (Hold on, wasn't this trip taken by boat? Didn't a suitcase fall off the roof of the car while driving out of Piraeus, clothes scattered all over the highway?)

Ninety-eight per cent of the population belongs to the Orthodox Church. Muslims, Roman Catholics, Protestants and Jews account for two per cent.

Watching a parade of guards. The infantry. The navy.

An olive tree at Olympia, woman posing at the start line, children already racing.

Do we deserve this?

Boy clutching promotional postcard stands alongside another boy, a popular act in a travelling circus from Russia.

Daddy, Why did you Call me Bastard

(I'll tell you if you really want to know…)
Her T-shirt said 'Kiss me, I'm Irish' but her talk
was funny, you know, not from these parts.
She shouldn't have brought me to that show, I didn't understand
a word, it was all about her own kind of stuff.
Dinner cost me 40 Euro, so, really, for 40 Euro
she let me do more than kiss.

I'm not a historian! That's how I am –
either I forget at once or keep things in my head
forever. Or make them up. She screamed
she'd put you up for adoption. Well, I couldn't have that.
So I gave her a few smacks
but after, when I saw her dangling you over the canal,
I flipped. I thought she'd get wet by the splash.

1 July 2010

Nothing

Nothing brings about moral downfall like
the permanent fear of a downgrade.
A down-and-out is the talk

of the town, and so is this mild weather we are having and how
the threat from outsiders has been weathered.
But on whether we'll survive

the recession the jury is still
in recess – which seems to last for as long
as the recession itself

will take to blow over.
Blow me if I care, I yelled at my colleague last night,
and if we come to blows over this

it'll be a crying shame. An old woman nearby
said shame on you to talk
like that, you shame your country

as well as your family. Her argument rang
familiar: it issued from the annals
of history. Family or country:

the locals have their loyalties
mixed up. Courses in local history
are located around the county

like the cherry blossoms in this premature spring
that haven't put a spring in my step (just yet).
I could barely leave the bedsprings

this morning as I anticipated the church
yard full with people in mourning
over the latest death. Morning!

chirps the health freak jogging
straight into the coffee shop. He jokes that if he's to stand
before some joker of a god he'll make sure

to get cupfuls of great
tea first. Mine's the cup of lapsang souchong,
I admit, and cup

my hands in a clumsy gesture of thanks
as I hand the waitress my loyalty
card. Hands off my breasts –

not here! she signals to the freak. I return to my room
where I get to work: I make room on the bed
and lie next to my roommate

thinking of her. I touch myself
with her cold fingers and sigh
at her sweet memory and feel the rush

of her final words wash
over me. In a word: ecstasy.
And if you think this is all just wordplay

16 X 16

I would have been a completely different person without the
      politics and a completely different **writer**.

Would a person have been different completely without the
      politics, and I, a writer, completely **different**?

Have I been completely a different writer without the politics?
      And would a different person **completely**?

Been completely different without the writer. Would I have a
      different politics completely? And person **A**?

A different person would have been completely without the
      writer, a different "I" politics (completely), **and**...

Completely a different person have I been; and the writer
      would—without a completely different **politics**.

Different politics completely would have a completely different
      writer. And I been a person without "**the**".

Person A would have been completely different: a writer. The
      politics different completely. And I **without**!

Without a completely different politics, the writer and I would
      have been completely a different **person**.

The different "I" politics, completely without a person and a
      writer, would have been completely **different**.

Politics would have been completely different without a writer and the"I"—a different person **completely**.

And, without politics, the person would have been completely different. I a different writer completely? **A**!

A different politics without the writer. Completely. And completely a different person, I would have **been**.

Completely been a different person. And I completely without the politics! Would a different writer **have**?

Different I have been. Completely. A different person. And, completely without the politics, a writer **would**.

Writer: without a politics, the person would have been a completely different... Different, completely! And **I**?

84

Dream with Jeff Koons and La Cicciolina

In their luscious garden they ask me
to join them for a threesome. She lies naked
and paleskinned with tight cherry-red nipples

and he leans on his elbow with his knee
bent, looks at me enigmatically, his hair dark
and neat. His cock is covered

with flowers. While we fuck I can't help thinking
how contrived all this is, like a prelude
to a business deal. He shuts

his eyes but does not convince: she at least can act
ecstasy. After we finish we have a picnic
on the grass. He grabs food from my plate. She spreads

her legs and flashes her knickers at me,
hair escaping the elastic rim
rebelliously. I'm told some find this

erotically charged. She hasn't waxed in months:
now she has a regular fuck she's beyond caring
about smoothness. Seduction is no longer

the game. She hands me a note, an invitation
to a performance, its tone formal
to the point of meaninglessness. I start to compose

a response when she gives me
another note with suggestions towards it. She says
we are telepathic. He still stares at me,

smirking. I remain unconvinced
about your role, he says, and puts his hand
on my groin. She whips out a camera-phone. We kiss.

I try to mess up his hair but it's impossible,
and he pushes me away. Later in her car
she exhibits daredevil skills, but this too I reckon

is an act. Back at her palace
he is stroking her blonde locks. She is lying on white sheets,
nipples expanded and aggressive, and he holds her

tight, his leg knocking the door shut in my face.

Ne Me Quitte Pas

Nor so was a gave it what she I'll sign I'll give   moment my life
is waiting to be decided   I'd told I need all this through   have
been still shares plans, dreams unlocked being heart and she went
this woman email   opened up in but it must be from them but
eight happy but all   together. I've been in this, so very special
years, that she risks based on something very nervous of   Hi,
well, I project I brother we are in worthwhile try to enjoy   for
her to come at risk and 5.48pm   always been ed. If I can for us
commitment rowing out of so short-lived someth   yahoo.com
29, 2013   strong, happy that with we'd finally to try to this. It's a
confusion   is almost she's caused me so stake. If there's any
hopeful but not   come op and I have few days with of very regul
print cut up over for time to sort email right   upon and chose
what's going und to want to So she should   its and promises
window for in an exciting and seemed to   much, too her as well
shit ago. But really and process because she   believe). A I hope
we before) and to the next I've certain were mad   I'd built a it's
a frig by now will soon) old man now hope – it's the things   life
through relationships   if you don't mind   happiest man in
embracing the way now that the doms left unused, bits ever since
shortly after her act, she feels she   are both real – even loving.
So far with three days toge   too much the moment   To Date
seems ab though it do can work if an emotion stage of our had
enou and a life   on at all and sho   'in love' but sure of
anything rather as so through all   sent from and just ok. Don –
hing   I'm son – and ever seen anything   Love to all week (a
trying to but sleepless a couple of lo ther on Wed think we've
you'll be aware that I'd be and whole world, which or rejected –
borne of a and support, that complete world: decision (mostly is
pretty folic acid bough she first told me return it was I've   spark
a few years her head out my nose –   king vulnerable in the park
she's used feels and off now. You a ring   hate her foe ply and
there as me (I am, at   cape and give it Hell we've bee – level
except before   confused at the mom than sexually – nor wanted
this, that we can   uch pain and hope I must. I've   ship with
perhaps emotional... I've gone from admire with all few weeks
before alanced   ded to call you you – but we it's my life at the
the balance,   something unfamiliar have   I know you

compared that time to   eave that lab etc risked ever keep hold
felt so   print both saw me this. She asked me develop this
'affair' I'm waiting   about blank our of and leave ything – I and
try to separate   even relation (was And love only a heads   best
man as you know been a sad normally do to tender   on right now
is the flat I've But I can't. I can't   as i uld maybe just short of a
few   my iPhone going through) tions we are doing back to
London to suspect   Sunday, at the mo   lives together and
learned and love built sign   be true to her we are back   it so
much use it to take u before by rel   I can't go love that   easy
and I do the same deep love and mutual care over there in
gnment she'd something snapped sometimes I worked on so
happened someone I made a baby – long and at first now after a
that love her too be strong   about the poetry that big sorry to go
on but that relationship is very painful   out these feelings neither
is specific   difficult We parents thin she says   her sexuality
seem very (I've barrier   But it is with you   subject from that
this. I can't help   he I   painful after just few week (though
them ong-term and a here was still soly messed her up in my
driven by her) done (togeth etc! And now of her 'emotion' become
attra   all a rest   she obviously place on an assign

Public Announcement

text 1

meltdown
in 5 minutes
but shutdown doesn't come

public fear
if not fullform anger
            grows

a game of impressions
and multiple threats
(after all what's life
imitating chess
but this)
            begins
– start white's clock –
though it's pointed out
it's always
            ticked on

a mathematical mind
constructs a queuing system
            beep!
ticket no. 88 goes to counter
to counter terrorism
charges from the bank
            counter-
litigation is fear
is
            migration

informality to military
tones
(note: In English first, then As Gaeilge)
            Skerries / Na Sceirí
            Malahide / Mullach Íde
notorious-

ly upper middle
class if not quite West
Brit but Gael-
scoil snob

                    migration

dialect to basic English
                    – Bases Out! –
to Mother Greek
and back
and forth
                    Leoforos Tzon Kenenty
                    Odos Fragklinou Rousvelt
ethno-political correctness disappearing
up its own arse

places
re-translated
back
                    back to
re-translated
places

warning!
in 2 minutes
file along
                    and pray
your reserved seats
aren't already occupied

                    fear
the bother
(don't make a fuss)

train approaching!

a thin yellow line now
separates you
from a surprising
                    Enterprising
crash

library cutups

you're turned off
the use of material obtained by mobile
means charging
50c for a read
as easy as this   better take one
photocopy it please deposit
in a library safe   a turnoff place
not only a bank holiday   it will charge
your will   your resolutions   it will
take you just beyond where
you're entitled

you're never far from another
in privacy

an office
closed for the centenary
give us celebrations we'll reopen
rooms for large communities
only book your magazines on confidentiality issues
at 2pm   no information supplied
no matter how courteous this alphabetised
promotional material
suggests   new books
installed or used by committee
a centenary of deposits?
please!

there's fiction in Braille
is a non-seen fact there   only
if faced by staff within the confines
of our clock

information makes citizens join
crime promptly
staff with regard to policy
are served   charged
with bulletin change three times

an hour

computer batteries to be marked by tower
tickets are required to board
phone and reserve

fact is a novel way to distribute
the here and now   available
at 5pm before mobile printing
is closed
phone for bookfire   yes
the story of languages and their evolution
included at all times

due care
please!
to be with teens
what is the point   even
in friendly manner
the book will be thrown
in this environment   climate
everywhere towns obsessed with tidy
adults   the council
must protect traditions

all libraries
signed with Irish blood   a fiction
is as good a consultation as you'll ever get
at this point   wait until Tuesday
when at least some information will be accepted
in print   online   no talking

our communication forms
have changed
if you're looking to return   to language
relevance   go online
the mind is opening
– I will say it twice, opening –
on Friday

for your reference all libraries   are best
manned by staff with knowledge

& application   turned
between policy on the one hand
and lunch
please!
while away the time here you're in
for a treat

public-private

in collaboration with James Wilkes

Tunnel operation reversed: plan ahead Murphy: inspire a
DETROIT generation: 9pm to 6pm: wildcats, roadworks

have the funeral of your choice @ camden / hands free set on bus /
between 5th and 9th any day / what's so hard to understand / your
stupid

no toilets in library what a dickhead librarian no customer service /
this male staff member is a dick head you should not work here get
out

Like a 4-pinter that works well it lasts but if the crap falls in it
sends the whole bottle bad that happened once and in like 2 days it
was bad & full of crap

@wilkesjames It's a song without title / things you treasure that
you never had / news circled the world / go swim in the sea here at
home

@c_makris felt there was a massive profit margin / with a negative
view, as they were getting deployment / this is a massive contract /
yes

Have your say in the strongest possible terms / boycott Mauritius
holidays now register for your household charge account /
penalties apply

I think they will regret it / sharply / an inquest unlawfully killed /
misconduct unenviable & property slumps / people who voted
Conservative / eroded

@c_makris featuring most famous artists of the / rhubarb
processor a pin verified dichlorobenzyl alcohol / a disciplinary
record / apology

@wilkesjames Forgotten something? Clean up / keep up the boycott don't be bullied / authorised vehicles only / commuter lifestyle encourages

The illuminati is bent / fuck off skaters / were still gonna come up here / were watchin / spell properly man

@c_makris bias in marking stung by cost / blind marking exists / the liberal democrats are way off beam / is this science my lords / offset

@wilkesjames media attacks the left / why so serious / student rail hate to live here / whats the independents agenda / the comfort movement

Chinooks ruined the film and / 2 sets of values / shorelines is watchin / the longshot / on my next / c'mon / UCH UCH

@c_makris who brings a knife to a fishfight / who dares jeans / who put the custard in the Rhinewald / was it @c_makris in the library

I think she's a bit like marmite to West Byfleet / my schizophrenic friend, who lives in America. He's a lovely guy, but I can't see him ever having a job. Good

@c_makris dont type so fast blud / so u best pray we got jobs. At any time suffering serious caffeine blowout & looking to buy in your area!

@wilkesjames out of order vandalism / the spanish man knows / hello I'm from Ukraine / the arab's busy / not in eastern europe? / na zdrowie

I'm in napa bitch / waiter or waitress wanted experience / shift morning or night freshly squeezed / glass bottom boat / other trush

@wilkesjames karaoke free viagra if you sing / leads to longlife / for your safety do not walk through the barrier walk around it

Hear a real story of a man who was born and lived / occupied ghost town / tonight comedy hypnotist Michael Jackson / all in the charcoals

Is this the cherty bed? Why not indulge yourself in a delicious cream tea DO NOT USE IN EYES OR ON GENITALS

@wilkesjames I want to do a jesse / follow the frog / we compine the old methods with the modern technology / our products are produced

This water is spring 2km from here don't worry is clean / fully furnished for girls or couple / goods in the base of the diet

@wilkesjames Trade your item for cash then buy it back in 28 days / closed due to continuous non-payment of rent and breech of a court order

Ali's hen weekend Dublin 2012 / a champion is someone who gets up when he cant / you can help stop this visit / 405 new missed calls

I <3 ADMIN and Jon <3s portables like (koff) / wassa hen do? You'll do no such thing / lays eggs. Or in my branch of Morrison's a crow was flying. Dirty crow.

@c_makris consequently I bought a diesel off of TA, the same fish salesman which owned the Golden Spray. I bought it off them for 100 quid

Im leading a fast life because Im in love with Agnes / you think it rains a lot in England but it doesn't. So I think there's a lot of people come in on trains

I still say my prayers every evening - before I go to bed / at like 3 o'clock on the morning, wearing all his clothes / if you're looking 4 devotion

@c_makris we also have the Hello magazine and other light refreshments / and of course cash thankyou.

@wilkesjames how can we defeat austerity / need to hire a coach? / customers wanted apply within / dress for the official handover of goats

If we forget for a moment about political correctness is there any of us who'd live next door to travellers / seats are not for fees

@wilkesjames home helps care workers demonstrate / sword sex press / sorcha and bryan wedding / every child matters / cigarette ends please

@wilkesjames broadband more important than electricity / the alternative to capitalist crisis / anti-climb paint applied to this drainpipe

Children should be seen and heard / tattoo piercing / an element of undesireables on the train / a bunch of posers / vote yes

Garda martina noonan gets done by a dog / she had a heartbeat too / something nice and irish / grit salt no shit / no Dublin city sewage

@wilkesjames this is a catholic country / this is a catholic country / this is a catholic country / this is a catholic country / this is a c

@c_makris GREAT CHOICE! Energizer Carabiner LED Area Tent Light- Idol Classifeds - Got it. Flaunt it!

@c_makris Goodbye responsibility carabiner, hello good times carabiner!

@c_makris Can we all stop fooling around & admit that "lanyard" & "carabiner" are super weird words that sound like they were made up by the

@c_makris I wish I were indoors. At least Burger King has free wifi. I need a carabiner for my keys. Maybe I can find one on Kijiji or Craig

@c_makris gaming the ring-fence, a makeshift group of Christians, Communists and Sunni Nigella's chocolate Guinness cake.

Notes

Metro Herald's Advertorial Wind Bags Let Loose, 28-31 May & 4-7 June 2013
Composed out of advertisements and 'letters to the editor' published in Dublin's free *Metro Herald* newspaper over the periods mentioned in the title.

Heaney after Rauschenberg
All four-letter words in Seamus Heaney's book *Death of a Naturalist* (Faber & Faber, 1966) in order of their appearance in the text.

Chances Are
For an online application of this mass collaboration poem go to http://www.3ammagazine.com/3am/chances-are/ .

Live the Life
An adaptation of a question-and-answer voiceover monologue in Jean-Luc Godard's film *Vivre Sa Vie* (1962).

Let It Play: An Improvisation
Live-written during Peter Michael Hamel's improvised composition/performance/lecture at St Patrick's College, Dublin, on 14 March 2005.

take the word butterfly
A response to an interview question from Dimitra Xidous for the project 'The Ash Wednesday series: How to Speak Poetry'.

Genius or Not
Seven pieces written under the constraints of the Genius or Not project – stipulating that each participating writer produce a text of not more than twenty lines or five hundred words, the content of which would not be preconceived in any way, at least once a month and within a period of one hour. The project, managed by Anthony Banks and running for one year as an online coda to *Succour* magazine, took inspiration from Harry Mathews' 'Twenty Lines a Day' exercise from 1980.

From Something to Nothing
The 'about' text on the International Monetary Fund (IMF) website
run through eight European languages, back and forth four times,
on Google Translate.

Prime Time
A live transcription of all advertising broadcast on Ireland's state
TV channel RTÉ1 between 6pm and 11pm on Friday 28 February
2014.

Why I live in Egypt
The initiating text was extracted from the article 'Why I live in...
Egypt' published in *The Irish Times Magazine* on 23 August 2003.

Civilisation's Golden Dawn: A Slide Show
Two of the entries are translations of a public, multi-phobic rant by
an MP from Greek neo-fascist party Golden Dawn, as provided by
two separate online translation engines.

Daddy, Why did you Call me Bastard
Composed out of fragments overheard around Dublin on 1 July
2010.

16 X 16
The line that forms the basis of the piece is taken from an
interview with the writer Rebecca Solnit as published in *The
Guardian* on 29 June 2013.

Public Announcement
library cutups
A transcript of all signage displayed in Skerries public library in
Co Dublin on Friday 4 May 2012, cut up and rearranged.

public-private
An exchange conducted between CM and James Wilkes through
Twitter and SMS over the second half of 2012, consisting of
fragments from public announcements of all kinds.

Made in the USA
Charleston, SC
09 March 2015